A Yankee's Guide
to Surviving Life in the South

and

A Southerner's Guide
to Surviving Life with Those Damn Yankees

by Kate Dyer

authorHOUSE®

AuthorHouse™
1663 Liberty Drive
Bloomington, IN 47403
www.authorhouse.com
Phone: 1-800-839-8640

This is an AuthorHouse book.

This edition published in 2012 by
AuthorHouse

Published by AuthorHouse 1/8/2013

ISBN: 978-1-4817-0586-8 (sc)
ISBN: 978-1-4817-0585-1 (e)

Library of Congress Control Number: 2013900367

creative support & design
© 2012 by Dana Dyer Pierson
Renaissance Woman Designs

A Yankee's Guide
to Surviving Life in the South

and

A Southerner's Guide
to Surviving Life with Those Damn Yankees

by Kate Dyer

PART ONE
A YANKEE'S GUIDE TO SURVIVING LIFE IN THE SOUTH

FOOD FOR THOUGHT: A TASTE OF THE NORTH
Or, A Little Yankee Home Cooking

APPETIZERS, BREADS, AND DIPS

SOUP AND SANDWICH

VEGETABLES

SEAFOOD

POULTRY AND PASTA

...AND EVERYTHING ELSE

"A SIMPLE MEAL"

CLASSIC NEW ENGLAND LIBATIONS

PART TWO

A SOUTHERNER'S GUIDE

TO SURVIVING LIFE WITH THOSE DAMN YANKEES!

FOOD FOR THOUGHT: A TASTE OF THE SOUTH

Or, How a Yankee Learned to Cook Like Y'all Do

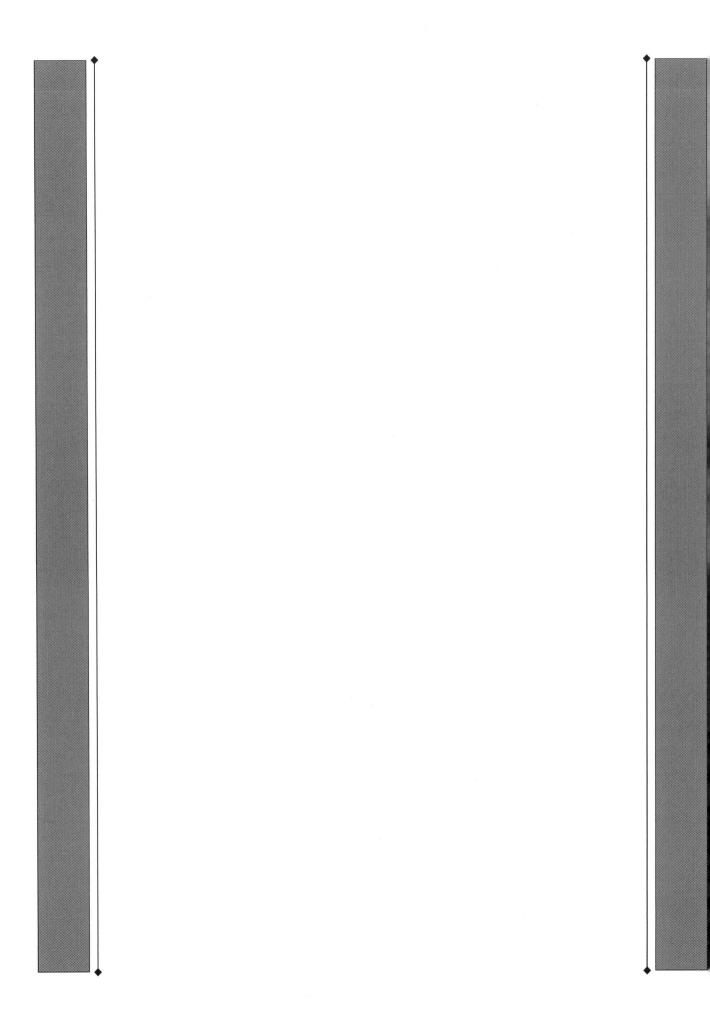

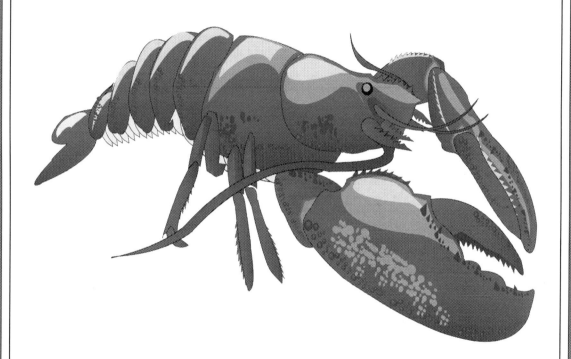

A Yankee's Guide

to Surviving Life in the South

Introduction

Let's start with the basics: *I am a Yankee, Boston-born and bred.*

In 2005, through a series of uninteresting events, I ended up in the mid-South, in a rural community north of Nashville, Tennessee. I am a lawyer by trade, on the wrong side of fifty, opinionated and blunt. I'm also a WOMAN! So I figured these Southerners would either love me or hate me, and my legal practice would either thrive or flop. Well, after a few years in practice here, I can honestly say that on the whole, the people here have been wonderful to me. I have been very successful in my law practice, but that doesn't mean I don't miss my Yankee home.

So during the holidays, I began to think about the tastes and scents and culture of home. (Yes, Southerners, we Yankees DO have culture!) Once I began comparing notes with a few other Yankees living here, the idea of this little missive was born. Both Yankees and Southerners will laugh at times (and yes, you'll both likely be mystified by some things too). Hopefully, at the very least, everyone will like some of the recipes.

As much as I love living here, sometimes I still miss the tastes, sounds, and sights of my New England roots. No matter where you live, if it's not where you grew up, there are still those things that remind you of childhood, of good times, of HOME ... and I've gathered some of those memories for you here.

I've also assembled some of my favorite recipes. Some are mine and others are borrowed (with kind permission) from friends and relatives. To start, in part one of my book— *A Yankee's Guide to Surviving Life in the South*—I've included some classic Yankee recipes. For those who have relocated to the South and miss classic Northern tastes, these recipes can serve as a survival guide to the homemade tastes of home.

I've also included a few tried-and-true Southern recipes I've learned to love, for those who want to try their hands at the homemade tastes of their *new* home. These are some of the classic Southern recipes this "Goddamn Yankee" (more on that in a minute) has learned to make in an attempt to at least TRY to assimilate into the local culture.

In part two of my book— *A Southerner's Guide to Surviving Life with Those Damn Yankees*—I've done my best to demystify the baffling Yankee species. Southerners, listen up: You'll learn a bit about what makes your neighbors from the North (and I ain't talking about Canadians, y'all!) tick. We, like you, have our own language. I thought y'all might enjoy learning a bit more about what life here in the South is like—from a Yankee's perspective.
And once you start to understand us, maybe you'll even come to love the next damn Yankee you meet!

And just to keep things fun, I have added a few stories and a jokes.
May you enjoy reading it as much as I enjoyed writing it.

- Kate

Life in the South: A Yankee Transplant's Perspective

Living in the South has been a sometimes strange and sometimes hilarious experience. One of the first things I learned early on in living here is that while it happened more than 150 years ago, "The War of Northern Aggression" may be gone—but it will never be forgotten.

Southerners have a unique way of letting a person know that "they ain't from here." Generally, the newcomer—no matter if they hail from California or Maine—gets labeled as not just a "Yankee," but a "Damn Yankee."

The difference?

A "Yankee" is a Northerner who comes here, spends money,
improves the economy ... and then goes home.

A "Damn Yankee" is one who comes ... and stays.

After living here for eight years or so,
I have coined my own term for Yankees like me:
a "Goddamn Yankee."

A "Goddamn Yankee" is a Yankee who came here,
likes it here, is staying here, but is still proud to be a Yankee.
And if YOU don't like THAT, there's the goddamn door!
(I can't tell you how many times that has broken the ice for me.)

Another fascinating thing about life in the South is a common ritual you'll encounter whenever you meet a new person. After they ask your name, they immediately ask you where you go to church. Now, if you are like me, you DON'T go to church—and admitting that can be deadly in these parts. The obligatory church invite is automatic (and weeks of follow-up are a given). So I figured I had better come up with a better answer.

When asked this particularly invasive, ill-gotten, and none-of-your-damn-business question, I look the person straight in the eye as I tell them where I go to church.

"Well, it depends on the Sunday," I explain with a smile. "Sometimes, I go to Bedside Baptist with Pastor Pillow and Reverend Sheets, and some Sundays, I go to The Church of the Master Bedroom, where all you can hear is "Oh God! Oh God! OOOH GAWD!"

That usually shuts them up.

Oh yeah—I NEVER invite them to MY church.

One of the reasons we moved to the South, after a number of winters in New Hampshire, was for the proverbial "better weather." Now I understand the Northeast gets cold. I understand that it snows in the winter and is hot in summer. But Tennessee is the only place I know that if you come here for "better weather," you better have a good snow shovel ... a storm shelter for tornadoes ... and flood insurance! And don't forget a good air conditioning unit.

There's no Cape Cod here to escape to!

Yankee Ingenuity

Let's move on to Katie's helpful hints. Well, not just Katie's. To be fair, I stole most of them from family and friends, but some are original, born of necessity.

Yankee ingenuity at its finest.

Now, if you are like me, you are busy and may even tend to be disorganized. Here are some helpful tips I have learned over the years from both Yankees and Southerners. I hope they make your life just a LITTLE easier!

FOR THE KITCHEN ...

When you buy a large amount of frozen chicken breasts, you can save both room in the freezer and time by prepping the exact amount you normally need for a single serving. Whether that's one or six, set up a single-serving portion in a large freezer bag. Then, when it's time to cook, you just grab one of these smaller-portion bags, not the whole ten-pound package they came in! (This took me until age fifty-three to figure out.)

Snip the cooking instructions off of the larger package of any frozen food you buy regularly (chicken breasts, hamburger patties, etc.) and tape it inside the cover of a favorite cookbook or pantry door. This way, you always have a copy to refer to when cooking. This will save you from either dangerously overcooked or undercooked meat in the future.

Even easier, if you are putting the chicken in the baggie, add the cut out directions into the baggie right away. Handy!

Do you ever buy a box of frozen something and you don't use all of it, but the half-full box takes up a HUGE amount of space in the freezer? Here is a solution: Take the remaining fish sticks, frozen hors d'oeuvre, whatever, and put them in a baggie. Cut off the cooking instructions, fold them up and put them in the bag. Recycle the big box and save room in the freezer.

Pull all the spices out of your spice cabinet, and make an alphabetical list of them. Scotch tape the list to the inside of the cupboard where you keep your spices. That way, you always know if you have a spice you need. Or impress your friends that you have them. (The spices, not friends.)

When you cut up onions, have a used baggie handy. Put the unusable parts all together in the baggie as you chop it. Then, zip the baggie closed and throw it away. Now, you'll be free from these odors until you take the trash out!

Got too many cookbooks? (Not that this is MY issue, but I figure SOMEONE might!) Take a weekend afternoon, and go through them and find your favorite recipes. Have a glass of wine while you are doing this. (Trust me; it helps.) Type them up, scan them (on another day, depending on how much wine you have had), and save them on your hard drive. Now, you can give away or sell the cookbooks. If you sell them, use the money you earned to replace the wine you drank!

Use the recipes that are in this book. Most are easy, affordable, and may be recipes you've never tried if you are a Southerner. Trust me. They are all great. I am the world's PICKIEST eater; I KNOW these things! ENJOY!

Got a favorite wine bottle from a special occasion? Don't throw it away! Wash it out, sign and date the label, and throw all your loose change in it during the course of the year. On the next special occasion, you will have money to celebrate with! Yet another reason to drink wine!

Speaking of wine, if you are classy like me, you drink wine in a box. Once the wine is gone, take the plastic bag out, and rinse it out. Deflate it and put it away until you have to pack boxes with fragile stuff. Just blow them up like a balloon! They can be re-inflated to whatever size you need. Best of all, you won't have to mess with those annoying "ghost poop" Styrofoam things that get everywhere. Look how environmentally friendly you are. (Don't forget to recycle the box itself, too.) Just a few more good reasons to drink wine!

Got stale bread? Before it turns moldy, make croutons with it! Brush each slice with butter or olive oil, and season if you like. Bake on an ungreased cookie sheet at 250° for 15 minutes, cut into smaller pieces, and you have fresh croutons. Like or need bread crumbs? Pulse the baked bread for 30 seconds in the blender. Store in zipper baggies in the pantry for up to two weeks or in the freezer for up to three months.

This next bit is shared with a bit of tongue-in-cheek humility. I always considered myself a Yankee brainchild, but in this story, you meet my Yankee brain-dead child. Enjoy and learn:

In our family, cooks always cut off the ends of a ham before putting it into a pan. Why? No one knows. I do it … my mother did it … her mother did it … my sister does it … my aunts did it, but no one knew why we all did it this way.

One day, my cousin Ann decided to get to the bottom of things. She asked my then ninety-year-old grandmother why she cut the ends off of the ham before baking it. (I should add that my grandmother looked at my cousin as it she were insane for asking.)

And what did Nana say? What was the answer to the great family mystery?

"The only pan I had was too small to hold the big ham, so I cut off the ends to make it fit."

So what's the real lesson here? The real Yankee wisdom here? Don't just automatically do something your mother always did, your grandmother always did, the

church always did, without asking WHY they did it that way.
    And the moral? Maybe then you won't feel as stupid as I did that day.

FOR THE HOME ...

If you have a cat box, save the WalMart bags, and hang them in a bag holder above the cat box. Every time you need to clean the cat box, pull one down, clean the box, and knot the handles before throwing the bag in the trash. This keeps odors for escaping and cuts down on the clutter of WalMart bags! Can you think of a better use for WalMart bags than cat poop?

If you have an area of electrical cords in one place, get a wicker basket, pile the cords in it, and put pine cones or rocks or whatever you like on top of the cords. (And for the record, I didn't think of this. Kathy, my Southern cleaning lady, did. I stole it.)

Got a bunch of stuff you don't want that's too good to give to Goodwill, and you're too busy/lazy to have a garage sale? Plan a Saturday afternoon "Swap 'til Ya Drop" party. Everyone gets a ticket for each item them bring. Then, put numbered tickets into a bag, one for each guest. To determine who gets to "shop" first, draw a number from the bag. Each person then gets to pick one item per round. At the end of the day, box up everything and take it to Goodwill (or whichever charity you want to support). This is a win-win: You get things you no longer need out of the house, and everyone gets new treasures without spending any cash.

Every time you buy something new, put something you own of the same genre (clothes if you buy clothes, kitchen utensils if you buy kitchen utensils) in the Goodwill box. One in, one out. Make an appointment with yourself to deliver to Goodwill or have a swap party three times a year.

Like flowers but don't like to keep paying for them? Use silk flowers. They need no water, they don't die, you never have to throw them out, and you can make 'em smell good by spritzing them with whatever scent you are in the mood for today! And people are impressed that you have flowers!

WHEN YOU TRAVEL ...

When you travel, take the goodies from the hotel bathroom. When you get several groups, give them to the women's shelter. Costs you nothing and gives you the feel-goods.

Keep a cosmetic/personal care bag packed in your suitcase. One less step in the frantic last -minute packing frenzy. Plus, you don't forget anything! If you don't travel often, be sure to check expiration dates.

If you are flying, make sure that everything in your carry-on is allowed by the TSA. If not, security WILL confiscate your things.

FOR THE CAR ...

Do you ever get extra salt/ketchup/napkins at a fast food drive-thru? What happens to them? Do you throw them out? If you save them, do they end up all over your car? Here is an easy solution: Keep a small zipper baggie in your car, and keep it in the glove compartment. When you have drive-thru extras, put them in the baggie right away. No mess, no waste, and you're set for those times when drive-thru drops the ball.

Believe it or not, I learned this one while living in the South! Stuck in the snow or on the ice? Get those spinning tires moving! Get a bag of cat litter. When you are stuck, sprinkle it around the tires about an inch thick. The spinning tires will grab it and spread it under the tires, and off you go.

Living in the South, I get a lot of questions about winter driving. Here's my favorite: You know how dirty your car headlights get from slush? Before winter sets in, wipe your headlights with ordinary car wax. It keeps the mess from accumulating on the headlights, and you can see! This will keep your headlights clean for about six weeks.

Nothing is as annoying as sitting in your car in the cold, waiting for the defroster to clear your car windows after a heavy frost. To avoid this, fill a spray bottle with three parts vinegar to one part water, and spray on the windshield at night. In the morning, you'll be ice and frost free!

Ever been in cold so cold that your car doors freeze shut? (The Yankees are nodding here.) To prevent this, before winter, lightly coat the rubber door seals with spray cooking oil and rub it in with a paper towel.

Does your windshield ever get foggy? Prevent this by spraying shaving cream INSIDE on the windshield. Then, wipe it off with paper towels.

Got a frozen car door lock and no de-icer? Squirt a little hand sanitizer on the key itself and insert it into the frozen lock.

Do your windshield wipers ever squeal or streak? Wipe them with cloth saturated with either rubbing alcohol or ammonia. The result? Clear window thanks to quiet blades (and no need to replace them just yet).

FOR DEALING WITH BILLS AND JUNK MAIL ...

If you live in the country and pick up your mail at the side of the road with your car, here's a great tip to manage the mail. If you are anything like me, some of it ends up in your car. Here is my solution: Keep two bags in the car. As soon as the mail is in your hands, the junk mail goes in one bag and the good mail in the other. Throw the junk mail in the recycle bin as you enter the house, and put the good mail in its proper place.

Good news: There's really no need to look at mail every day. The bills can wait. Think about it: Why waste time looking at something over and over again? Assign a non-bill mail day, and open these things then. Then assign a weekly bill-paying day on which you deal with all the bills immediately. You'll save about an hour a week with this system!

As for bills, coordinate the due dates to fall mid-month. On the second weekend, set aside time on Saturday morning to pay bills, and prep them for mailing. Stamp them and put them in your car visor, and mail everything the next morning.

You also now have the option to pay some bills online or by phone. You don't have to think about it again, you save time, and you save money on postage. Doesn't sound like much? Look at it this way: Say you mail five bills a month at .44 each. That's $2.20 a month or $26.00 a year. But how many bills do YOU mail each month?

And while we are at it, look at the time you save once automatic bill pay is set up! Figure six minutes to open the bill, scan the bill, write the check, fill out the corresponding paperwork to send back, put it in the envelope, put a stamp on it, put a return address label on it, lick it, and mail it. Six minutes, five times a month is six hours of your life you'll never get back each year. How much is YOUR time worth?

Well, that's just a taste of Yankee ingenuity for you. There's plenty more where that came from—all you need to do is ask!

You Know You're a Yankee Living in the South When ...

As I've said, life in the Northeast is far different from life in the South. These next two sections will give you la little taste of what it means to be a Yankee—or a Southerner.

- The first thing someone says to you when you meet is "You're not from around he-ah, ahhh ya?"
- You know the difference between a Yankee, a Damn Yankee, and a God Damn Yankee.
- You are proud to be a God Damn Yankee, which makes you a God Damn Yankee.
- You know at least one person who has married a cousin.
- You don't laugh at Jeff Foxworthy ... because you see him every day.
- In January, when everyone else is in wool coats and boots, you go out in shirt sleeves, wondering what all the fuss is about.
- You shake your head when school is closed for five days ... because of two inches of snow.
- The kids are back in school before the Halloween decorations are out in stores.
- You understand that "grits" is not another name for Cream of Wheat.
- You also understand that "grits" can also mean "Girls Raised in the South."
- You know Waffle House only accepts cash.
- You know this because you have BEEN to a Waffle House.
- So you also know that Waffle House has an ATM.
- Eating at Sonic is no big deal.
- Someone tells you THEY are a Yankee (and that they're from Chicago).
- You know the difference between "Church of Christ" and "United Church of Christ" (and you could NEVER confuse the two).
- You try schedule a dinner party for a Wednesday night ... and no one comes (or calls).
- "Greens" doesn't mean beans, peas, and peppers.
- "Greens" means turnip, collard, and some other thing I never ate and can't recall.
- You try to buy wine on Sunday and can't (and don't understand why).
- But you CAN buy beer on Sunday (and don't understand why).
- You know the location of ten tobacco barns ... and have come to like the smell.
- You have called 911 to report a fire in a barn in the fall and no longer wonder why the dispatcher laughed at you.
- Tractors share the road with cars, but you are the only one aggravated.
- You know what and where the "Batman" building is (and think it is hilarious that it is called a "skyscraper")!

The Boston Memory Test

Or, A Southerner's Guide to Understanding Damn Yankees

Life in the South is completely different than life in Boston. While this page may only resonate with former Bostonians and some New Englanders, it may be a good icebreaker to use when meeting a Yankee. At the very least, you'll find a few hints to help you decipher what that Yankee's talking about.

You know you are from Boston WHEN:

- You get all the Jewish holidays off from public school.
- You can name ten Dunkin Donuts, all within five blocks of each other.
- You know what the red, orange, blue, and green lines are … and have taken them.
- You know WHY Charlie can't get offa that train!
- You probably know where Scollay Square Station was (depending on your age).
- You know what Charleston Chews are … and where the factory is.
- You know where "Meffa" is next to Malden (and that the rest of the world pronounces it as "Medford").
- Your mother's sister is your "ahhhhhnt," not your ANT.
- You still call I-95 "128."
- You can smell corned beef and cabbage just thinking about it.
- You wouldn't be caught dead eating Manhattan clam chowder.
- Jordan Marsh will always be your favorite department store Santa.
- Remember Turnstyle? Raymond's?
- You know where the REAL Kelly's is!
- You know the difference between clam strips and fried clams!
- You eat oyster crackers and soda crackers.
- You know what a "fluff-a-nutah" is.
- You took your clothes off in the middle of Filene's Basement (to try ON clothes).
- A "regular" cup of coffee is with cream and sugar.
- You got in trouble for sharing your baloney sandwich with your Catholic buddy on Friday.
- You know that lettuce and tomato DO NOT belong on subs!
- You know Santoro's.
- You skated at an MDC rink (and paid 10 cents for the privilege).
- There is no way in hell you would climb Bunker Hill Monument!
- You offer someone a pronged eating utensil … and they think it is a sexual come-on!

- You understand that "wicked" actually means "extremely."
- You go to a restaurant and ask what kind of tonic they serve, and the waitress says Coke.
- You call your mother "MMMMaaaaaaaaaaaaaaaaa!"
- You understand the linguistic quirks of the area. You know that you aren't supposed to pronounce words ending in R or A as written. Just for fun, swap the two out: Hence, my college roommate Linda had to get used to being called "Linder." Thirsty? Then you'd best ask for a glass of "watah." Got it?
- You bought records at Lechemere Sales.
- You saw Betty on her Rolls Royce in the Everett Fourth of July parade.
- (And you probably threw peanuts in Betty's Rolls Royce, too).
- You won a pitcher of beer for singing all the words to "Charlie and the MTA" at BRR.
- You know the difference between a "milkshake" and a "frappe."
- You know what a "puker-pot" is.
- You can swear in English, Italian, and Yiddish, sometimes in the same sentence.
- You tell Midwesterners that eating "real" seafood means going down to the beach, twisting the snail off the huge rocks, and swishing it out in the incoming tide before putting it to your mouth so you can suck it out!
- You went to Revere Beach to ride the roller coaster.
- You spent your summers on the coast of Maine.
- You sat in the $2 bleacher seats at Fenway Park.
- The Southeast Expressway will always be the only way to the Cape.
- And you NEVER refer to the Cape as "Cape Cod."
- Fourth of July was spent on the Esplanade, listening to Arthur Fiedler, and watching the fireworks.
- And you got there by noon to get a seat on the grass (and didn't care if it rained).
- Going to the top of the Pru was a big deal.
- You remember the blackout of '67.
- You also remember the winter of '67, when there was no school for the entire month of February due to snow days.
- You played on the statues in "Gub-mit Centa" as a teenager
- And most importantly, you know you are from Boston if you "got" this list—and are damn proud of that fact!

FOOD FOR THOUGHT:

A TASTE OF THE NORTH

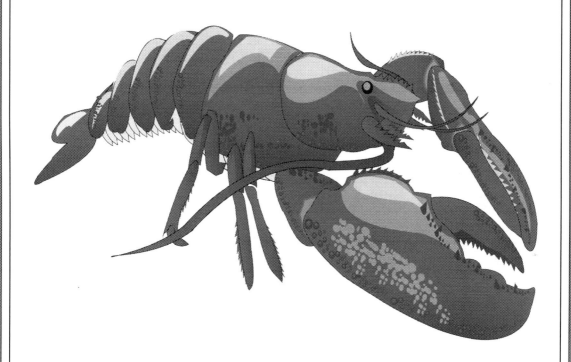

or

A Little Yankee Home Cooking

Rita's Rye Rounds

preheat broiler	prep five minutes	cook two to five minutes	yield twenty

1 loaf small rye cocktail bread (or Jewish rye cut into rounds)
8 ounces Cheddar cheese, finely shredded

1 cup Miracle Whip (not mayonnaise)
1 package real bacon bits (or 6 slices of bacon, crumbled finely)

In a bowl, combine cheese, Miracle Whip, and bacon bits; stir to combine.

Spread mixture onto bread.

Arrange rye rounds on a cookie sheet.

Broil for two or three minutes (or until cheese is bubbly and lightly browned).

Grandma's Date Nut Bread

| *preheat* 350° | *prep* fifteen minutes | *cook* one hour | *makes* one loaf |

1½ cups chopped dates
1½ cups sugar
1½ cups boiling water
1 teaspoon salt
2 tablespoons butter

2¾ cups flour
1 teaspoon baking soda
½ teaspoon vanilla
2 eggs, beaten well

In a medium mixing bowl, combine the dates, sugar, boiling water, salt, and butter; stir to combine.

Allow the contents to cool completely.

Once it's reached room temperature, stir in the remaining ingredients.

Pour into a greased bread pan and bake at 350° for one hour, or until a toothpick inserted into the middle emerges clean and dry.

Cool completely (assuming you can wait that long) and serve with butter and cream cheese.

Once Rita decided to cook, she decided to use her mother's recipes. And let me tell you, my grandmother really could cook! Her Date Nut Bread recipe is the ONLY recipe I have ever found that works every time.
I will never forget the first time I tried to make it. I was having my baby shower the next day, so I asked my mother for her mother's recipe.
I followed ALL the instructions exactly, but when I went to put the mixture in the bread pan, it was watery. What did I do wrong?

I had no clue, so I swallowed my pride about screwing up Rita's recipe and called my mom. She informed me I must have forgotten something. She asked me to read her the recipe. I did so, and as I got to the end, she was laughing so hard she was crying.
"You forgot to put the FLOUR in, you dope," said my uber-supportive mother.

To which I replied, "You forgot to add it to the RECIPE!"

I added the correct amount of flour, and guess what?

It worked.

Classic Crab Cakes

preheat 350°	prep 30 minutes	cook 30 minutes	yield 18 2" or 6 4" cakes

1½ pounds lump crab meat
4 ounces bread crumbs
2 scallions, diced
2 large eggs
1 tablespoon Old Bay™ Seasoning
Canola oil (for cooking)
Cocktail sauce
Lemon wedges

In a large bowl, combine bread crumbs, scallions, and Old Bay Seasoning; stir to combine.

Add enough oil to cover the bottom of frying pan to a depth of at least ½ inch. Heat the oil to approximately 350°.

In a smaller bowl, beat the eggs.

Add to the dry mixture. Mix with your hands.

Add the crab meat to the mixture, and mix with your hands.

For appetizer-sized cakes, take a small scoop (two tablespoons) and form into a small patty.

For entrée-sized cakes, divide the mixture into four or six equal parts.

Carefully add the crab cakes to the sauté pan, and cook for about two minutes on each side (or until golden brown and crisp).

Remove and serve with cocktail sauce and lemon wedges.

There are few New England appetizers more beloved (and in demand) than crab cakes.

The good news is that they are as easy to make as they are delicious.

You'll want to double or even triple this recipe if you're having company over.

Trust me: These will FLY off the buffet as soon as they are served!

Grandma's Mystery Dip

prep 5 minutes	*yield* 1 quart

1 16-ounce container of whipped cream cheese (at room temperature)
½ cup French dressing
Garlic powder (to taste)
Milk (as needed)
Vegetables or chips for dipping

In a medium mixing bowl, combine whipped cream cheese and French dressing.

Using an electric mixer, blend until light orange and smooth. If needed, use a little milk to get it to the consistency you like.

Add garlic powder (to taste).

Serve with sliced vegetables or chips.

Everyone loves this easy and delicious dip—and no one can figure out what's in it!

Be prepared: Everyone will ask for the recipe, but don't give it to them! This makes you much more mysterious (and they'll be sure to invite you to every party if they know you'll bring this with you)!

And I don't care how much they beg for the recipe … make 'em guess!

And no:

The titular lady in question is not my grandmother, but I know she's someone's grandmother …

New England Clam Chowder

preheat none	prep 20 minutes	cook fifteen minutes	serves 8

5 potatoes, diced
½ stick of butter, cut into small pieces
3 white onions, diced or grated
1 can Carnation milk
4 quarts whole milk
4 cans chopped clams, minced and rinsed (reserve juice)
2 teaspoons Old Bay™ Seasoning
Salt and pepper (to taste)
Oyster crackers or French bread

In a large soup pot, add butter and sauté until the potatoes are tender and the onions are lightly browned.

Add clams and reserved clam juice; stir.

Increase heat to bring juice back to the boil, then reduce heat.

Add milk (canned and whole); stir.

If you like it a little thicker, add roux (a gravy base made from flour). Lots and lots of butter will also improve the consistency.

Season to taste; stir.

Simmer for twenty minutes or so (or until the potatoes are fork-tender).

Do not allow to come to a boil again, and stir often to avoid scorching the soup.

Serve with oyster crackers or French bread.

*And now...
the recipe you've all
been waiting for!*

*So some have asked
me why Yankees
make such a big deal
about the difference
between New
England clam
chowder and
Manhattan clam
chowder.
Aren't they all the
same?*

No, NO, and NO!

*There are actually
two completely
different soups.
The only thing they
share, in my mind,
is clams.*

*New England clam
chowder (or,
"chowdah") is made
with cream and
potatoes and bacon.*

Bliss.

*Manhattan clam
chowder is red, made
with tomatoes, and
is an abomination.
I have never
tried it, and no
self-respecting
Yankee ever will!*

*As with New York
and Boston,
the two should
never be confused.*

"Jack Caraway" Sandwich

preheat broiler	*prep* 5 minutes	*cook* 2 minutes	*yield* one sandwich

4 ounces deli-style roast beef
Soft sandwich roll
3 ounces of sliced red pepper, sautéed
1 ounce sliced mushrooms (any), sautéed
1 ounce sliced onion, sautéed
2 ounces of Monterey Jack cheese, shredded
½ teaspoon caraway seeds

On a broiler-safe baking sheet, assemble sandwich by layering one ounce of Monterey Jack cheese, beef, and vegetables.

Add the remaining cheese and caraway seeds.

Broil for two minutes (or until cheese is bubbly and brown).

22

Okay, to be honest, I never had this as a kid.

John and I discovered this sandwich in a tiny sandwich shop in Bangor (pronounced "Bang-gah"), Maine. So it qualifies.

It's crucial that you use Monterey Jack cheese on this sandwich; no other cheese will provide you with the exact experience.

And trust me; it's worth it!

Nebraska Potatoes

preheat 350°	prep 5 minutes	cook 1 hour	serves 4

One bag O'Brien™ frozen potatoes, thawed
One 14-ounce can cream of chicken soup
16 ounces of shredded Cheddar cheese
8 ounces of sour cream (optional)
Salt and pepper to taste

Thaw a bag of O'Brien potatoes.

Put into the biggest casserole dish you have.

Add one can of cream of chicken soup.

Add as much finely shredded cheddar cheese as you like. I use the whole bag.

Add 1/2 container of sour cream. If you're worried about fat, you can either leave this out or use fat-free sour cream. The sour cream does add calories, but trust me, they're worth it!

Stir to mix.

Top with more cheese (optional)

Bake at 350° for an hour.

Broiler Room Potatoes

| preheat 350° | prep 10 minutes | cook 45 minutes | serves 4 |

3 large baking potatoes, peeled and thinly sliced
4 ounces cheddar cheese, grated
½ cup heavy whipping cream
Salt and pepper (to taste)
A few drops of Liquid Smoke™

In a small bowl, whisk the heavy whipping cream with Liquid Smoke.

Assemble as you would an au gratin: In a large, greased baking dish, alternate layers of potatoes and cream sauce. Season as desired.

Finish with a generous layer of shredded cheddar cheese.

Bake at 350° for one hour. If you like a crispier, more golden crust, pop it under the broiler for a few minutes just before serving.

I'm not quite sure why we took to calling this decadent dish by this name.

Perhaps the name was inspired by a similar dish we once had at a restaurant called the Broiler Room.

But that's just a guess...

But, boy oh boy, I don't care what you call them or why you call them that: just bring them on!

Kate's Most-Awesome Way to Eat Vegetables. Ever.

prep 10 minutes	cook 45 minutes	serves four

2 tablespoons extra virgin olive oil
3 cups vegetable mix, sliced (we use peppers, onions, mushrooms, etc.)
Minced garlic (to taste)
Salt and pepper (to taste)
¼ cup sour cream or ½ bottle Alfredo sauce
Fresh herbs (we use basil or oregano), minced
½ cup dry white wine
Olive oil

Heat oil in a medium frying pan.

Add vegetables and garlic, and sauté until soft, taking care not to let the garlic burn.

Add your choice of the sour cream or the Alfredo sauce; stir.

Add fresh herbs and wine; stir.

Let simmer on low for forty-five minutes; stir occasionally.

Season to taste with salt and pepper.

Yankee Fish

| preheat 350° | prep 5 minutes | cook 15 minutes | yield four |

4 Boston haddock (or other white fish) filets
1 sleeve Ritz crackers
Garlic powder (to taste)
½ cup butter, melted

If using frozen fish, thaw according to package directions.

Rinse fish with water, pat dry, and set aside on greased baking sheet.

To create the coating, start by putting the Ritz crackers into a gallon-sized freezer bag and seal well; crush with a rolling pin or your hands. You'll want a uniform, cornmeal-like texture.

Pour the coating into a large bowl and stir in melted butter and garlic powder (to taste).

Dip fish filets into coating mixture and place on greased baking sheet.

If you like your fish extra crispy, pat any additional coating mix onto the top of the fish.

Bake at 350° for fifteen minutes (or until the fish flakes with a fork).

Serve immediately.

So some nights, we got a break from chicken. We switched to fish (also cheap, especially if you got if right off the boat as we did).

Boston haddock is the most common white fish in New England, but cod, scrod, and halibut are almost as good. (This is not to be confused with catfish—as if anyone could!)

Here is THE easiest and best way to cook fish I know, in true New England style.

Frozen Boston haddock is available around the country, but fresh fish is always better, so work with that when you can.

Boiled Lobster

prep varies	cook 10 minutes	serves 1

One two-to-three-pound live Maine lobster per lucky diner
Melted butter

First, get your hardware organized, as you'll want everything ready to go the minute the lobster is ready to eat. For a proper lobster experience, you'll need (per diner) bibs, kitchen scissors, lobster/nut crackers, and seafood forks. And don't forget to provide plenty of napkins! It's also a good idea to have a community shell bowl to share.

In the biggest pot you have, bring salted water (2 quarts per lobster) to a hard boil. Be sure to leave plenty of room for the lobsters in the pot!

Pick the lobster up by the neck, using a towel to protect yourself both from the lobster and the boiling water.

Quickly drop the lobster into the boiling water, head first, and IMMEDIATELY cover the pot (otherwise, a half-dead lobster will try to climb out. Think I'm kidding? Skip this step).

Boil for five or six minutes or until the lobster has turned bright red.

With tongs, carefully remove the lobster from the pot, being sure to let any excess water drain into the pot.

Let the lobster rest for a few minutes. This will complete the cooking process and make it safer to handle as well.

As the lobster is cooling, melt the butter as needed.

Now comes the fun part—extracting the lobster from its shell! You have a few options. Lobster is a messy dish, so that's why you'll need the bib—and a big pile of napkins!
> You can break it open/apart with your hands.
> You can use the traditional lobster crackers (like a nutcracker, it's designed to crack or break the shell). This isn't as much fun as just tearing it apart, though.
> You can use sturdy kitchen shears to snip the shell open.

Once you've successfully freed the treasure, dip into melted butter, and enjoy.

Most people I talk to here in the South have never had a fresh lobster. They don't believe me when I tell them that we used to go to WalMart and get live lobsters for $2.99 a pound. They can't even fathom it.

The good news is that fresh lobster is now available in many parts of the country. Even if you can't get them fresh off the boat, visit the best fish market in your city and splurge every now and then. Just make sure the lobster is live; it makes a world of difference!

So, I guess this recipe is more for Yankees, or any Southerner fortunate enough to spend time in New England.

We had this about twice a week as a kid. Now, I won't eat it … so y'all can have my share.

Quahogs

preheat 450°	prep 20 minutes	cook 30 minutes	servings four

1 pound fresh quahogs (hard-shelled clams) or 2 cans minced clams (reserve juice)
2 tablespoons butter
1 large sweet onion, minced
¼ cup fresh parsley, stems removed and minced
parsley for garnish
2 cloves of fresh (not bottled) garlic, minced

1½ cups of seasoned bread crumbs
2 cups of clam juice (for use with fresh clams only. If you've used canned clams, use the juice from the can).
¼ teaspoon cayenne pepper
½ teaspoon paprika
¼ teaspoon onion powder
¼ teaspoon celery seeds
2 lemons, cut into wedges

In a food processor, prepare the topping: combine garlic, seasonings, and parsley with bread crumbs; process until the consistency of oatmeal.

Pour into a mixing bowl.

Add clams to the food processor bowl, and chop until coarsely ground; add to topping mix.

Melt butter; add to topping mix.

Slowly add clam juice and stir until mixture is moist, but not soupy. (If using fresh clams, add the bottled clam juice. If using canned, use the juice from the can.)

Lightly oil clam shells or ramekins (olive or peanut oil works best) and place on a lined baking sheet.

Fill shell or ramekin with mixture; sprinkle a generous amount of topping. with Bake at 450°F for 30 minutes or until centers are cooked.

To serve, sprinkle with a little fresh parsley and a lemon wedge.

Now this recipe is uniquely New England—and no, this ain't another name for chitlins! Quahogs ("kwo-hogs") are clams, and in this recipes, they are prepared in the shell, with spices and bread crumbs.

Despite their name, there is nothing "hoggish" about them. They are shellfish, so the REAL way to serve these is on clam shells. But, since clam shells are few and far between in the mid-South, you could use ramekins. They won't change the flavor, but it won't have quite the same impact on the eyes!

If you can find fresh clams, reach for this recipe! In a pinch, the canned ones will work. This is not the easiest recipe in the book, but I promise that it's worth it.

Besides, with a name like quahogs, it's an adventure from the get-go.

Sautéed Chicken in Wine Sauce

prep 15 minutes	cook 15 minutes	serves two

2 boneless, skinless chicken breasts (fresh or thawed)
1 egg
Panko bread crumbs (or Italian-seasoned bread crumbs)
Grated Parmesan cheese
Olive oil (for frying)
½ cup of white wine (or white cooking wine)
Salt and pepper (to taste)

Thaw two boneless, skinless breasts.

Whisk an egg in a bowl.

Mix Panko bread crumbs or Italian-seasoned fine bread crumbs with grated Parmesan cheese in another bowl; season to taste.

Cover the bottom of a large skillet with olive oil. Be careful not to let the oil burn as it heats, but it should be hot enough to sizzle when the food comes into contact with it.

As the oil is heating, dip the chicken first in egg, then in bread crumbs, coating each side.

Carefully place chicken in hot oil and brown each piece (two minutes each side).

Drain the oil from the pan and add ½ cup of wine; cover pan.

 Simmer over medium heat for fifteen minutes (or until chicken is cooked. Internal temperature should be 170°).

Remove chicken from pan, and pour a little wine into the pan to deglaze it. Scrape pan drippings from the bottom of the pan, and whisk to make a wonderful gravy!

Fancy-Schmancy Baked Chicken in Wine Sauce

| preheat | 350° | prep | 15 minutes | cook | 1 hour | serves | two |

2 boneless, skinless chicken breasts (fresh or thawed)
1 15-ounce can cream of celery (or cream of chicken) soup
1 cup Chardonnay (or any dry white wine)
2 slices Swiss cheese
1 cup Panko, Italian-seasoned bread crumbs, or Stove Top™ Stuffing

Place chicken breasts in a small in baking dish.

In a small bowl, whisk one can of cream of celery (or chicken) soup with the white wine.

Place a piece of Swiss cheese over each piece of chicken.

Pour soup mixture over chicken.

Sprinkle with Panko or Italian seasoned bread crumbs, or to be REALLY fancy, a cup of Stove Top™ stuffing.

Bake at 350° for about an hour (or until the chicken's internal temperature reaches 170°).

The most hilarious thing about this recipe is that when flipping through the cooking channels the other day, Paula Deen, the cooking goddess of Southern fare, was MAKING MY RECIPE.

If she only knew she was making a Yankee recipe!

God bless her heart!

Translation for Yankees:

"God bless her heart" means something considerably less charitable in most cases...

Broiler Room Chicken

preheat	350°	prep 15 minutes	cook 45 minutes	serves four

4 boneless, skinless chicken breasts
½ pound sliced deli ham
4 ounces Cheddar cheese, shredded
A few drops of Liquid Smoke™
½ cup heavy whipping cream

In a small bowl, combine whipping cream and three or four drops of Liquid Smoke; whisk to combine.

In a baking dish, assemble as if you were making Broiler Room Potatoes: Alternate layers of chicken, cream, ham, and shredded cheese.

Top with a layer of shredded cheese.

Bake at 350° for 45 minutes or until cheese is bubbly.

To confirm that chicken is fully cooked, pierce with a toothpick. If liquid runs clear, the chicken is cooked. The internal temperature should be 170°.

If you like a nice, brown crust, pop it under the broiler for a minute right before you serve it!

New England Boiled Dinner

prep 20 minutes	cook 2.5 hours	serves 6 to 8

3 pounds corned beef brisket
3 tablespoons pickling spices
3 bay leaves
6 black peppercorns
3 potatoes
3 carrots
1 onion, quartered
2 parsnips, cut into chunks
2 turnips, cut into chunks

1 small cabbage, cut into wedges
1 tablespoon salt

Horseradish Cream
1 cup sour cream
Prepared horseradish to taste
Salt and pepper (to taste)
Tabasco (to taste)

Make your spice bag by tying a piece of cheesecloth around the pickling spices, bay leaves, and peppercorns. Tie securely with cooking twine.

Add the meat and spice bag to a large soup pot and add enough water to cover the contents.

Bring to a boil, then reduce heat and simmer for two hours.

Cut potatoes, carrots, parsnips, and turnips into uniform chunks. Quarter the onion and cabbage; add to pot and stir well.

Simmer for an additional 30 minutes. Remove meat from pot and allow to rest for ten minutes.

As the meat is resting, make horseradish cream: In a small bowl, blend sour cream with up to 1 tablespoon prepared horseradish.
Season to taste with salt, pepper, and Tabasco.

To serve, move corned beef to platter and slice across the grain. Surround the meat with the vegetables and spoon a little of the broth over the top.

The remaining broth can be served as an *au jus.* It also makes an excellent soup base, so don't throw it out!

New England
Boiled Dinner
is as classic
a Yankee dish
as they come.

It's hearty, easy to
prepare, affordable,
and very satisfying
on cold winter days.

It's also a
great choice for
entertaining;
as all the work is
done ahead
of your guests'
arrival.

That way, you're
not chained in the
kitchen when they
arrive.

Turtle Noodles for Grown-Ups

preheat broiler	prep 20 minutes	cook 5 minutes	serves 4

1 package Velveeta Shells and Cheese™
1 teaspoon salt
2 tablespoons olive or canola oil
1 red pepper
1 green pepper
1 cup mushrooms, washed and sliced
¼ cup sun-dried tomatoes
½ cup cheddar cheese, finely grated
2 cups Panko bread crumbs (optional)
½ cup fresh Parmesan cheese

Bring a large pot of water to boil, adding 1 teaspoon of salt as it heats.

Prepare macaroni per package directions.

As the pasta is cooking, add olive oil to pan.

Sauté peppers, mushrooms, and sun-dried tomatoes until soft.

Once pasta is cooked, drain the water; return pasta to the pot.

Add the sautéed vegetables; stir.

Add ¼ cup cheddar cheese and the liquid cheese packet from the package; stir.

Transfer mixture to a greased baking dish.

If you want to really impress, top the pasta with the Panko.

Broil until the cheese is bubbly and lightly browned.

To serve, sprinkle some freshly grated Parmesan and pepper.

I will never forget a conversation I had with my daughter when she was about three years old. I asked her what she wanted for lunch, and she quickly said, "Turtle noodles." I had no idea what she was asking for. I told her that we didn't have any "turtle" noodles. "Yes, Mommy," Kaitlyn insisted, pointing into the pantry, "we do."

With the unshakable, rational confidence of an adult who knew that there absolutely no "turtle" noodles in my pantry, I picked her up and asked her to show me where they were. Kaitlyn then triumphantly pointed right at an infamously bright orange box of Velveeta Shells and Cheese. "See?" she announced proudly. "Turtle noodles!" And you know, as soon as she said that, I was able to see them as she did. And they really DO look like turtles! Now, twenty-five years later, we still keep "turtle" noodles in our house, but we dress them up a bit (so as to not make us look like the kids we really are at heart).

Fancy-Schmancy Gourmet Turtle Noodles

preheat broiler	prep 20 minutes	cook 5 minutes	serves four

1 package Velveeta Shells and Cheese
1 teaspoon salt
2 tablespoons olive or canola oil
1 red pepper
1 green pepper
1 cup mushrooms, washed and sliced
¼ cup sun-dried tomatoes
½ cup cheddar cheese, finely grated

½ cup feta cheese, crumbled
½ cup mozzarella cheese, shredded
2 cups Panko bread crumbs (optional)
½ cup fresh Parmesan cheese
Fresh oregano or basil, minced

Bring a large pot of water to boil, adding 1 teaspoon of salt as it heats.

Prepare macaroni per package directions.

As the pasta is cooking, add olive oil to pan.

Sauté peppers, mushrooms, and sun-dried tomatoes until soft.

In a small, microwave-safe bowl, combine the liquid cheese packet from the package, ¼ cup of the cheddar cheese, the feta, and the mozzarella; stir.

Heat the cheese sauce mix in the microwave until it resembles soup; stir again.

Once pasta is cooked, drain the water; return pasta to the pot.

Add the sautéed vegetables and cheese sauce; stir.

Transfer mixture to a greased baking dish. Since the goal here is to really impress, top the pasta with the Panko and the remaining cheddar cheese.

Broil until the cheese is bubbly and lightly browned.

To serve, sprinkle some fresh herbs, freshly grated Parmesan, and pepper.

Once you've make Turtle Noodles, you'll love them.

So it only makes sense you'd want to share them, right?

So here is a version we came up with that's more than fit for company!

This basic recipe should be just that: a base.

Have fun and be creative to create your own version.

American Chop Suey, Yankee Style

prep 10 minutes	cook 15 minutes	serves 6

6 cups water
1 box elbow macaroni
¼ teaspoon salt
1 pound good hamburger
¼ cup onions, diced
1 can stewed tomatoes
1 cup milk
1 cup ketchup
1 can tomato soup

1/8 cup tomato juice or V8
Fresh Italian or French bread
Parmesan cheese

Spices to taste, including Old Bay™
Seasoning, oregano, salt,
and pepper

Bring a large pot of salted water to a boil; add elbow macaroni and cook to desired tenderness.

As the pasta is cooking, sauté hamburger and diced onions.

Drain fat from the pan.

Add stewed tomatoes and stir; allow to heat thoroughly.

Add milk and cooked macaroni; stir.

Add ketchup, tomato juice/V8, and tomato soup; stir.

Season to taste; stir.

Reduce heat to low and simmer for up to two hours, stirring every thirty minutes or so.

If it appears to be drying out, add more tomato juice. Make sure the heat is low and steady, otherwise this one's going to become a Cajun dish (by which I mean *blackened*, cha).

To serve, ladle into bowls, garnish with Parmesan, and serve with warm bread.

Linguini with Artichokes & Prosciutto

prep 10 minutes	cook 5 minutes	serves 4

8 ounces linguini

2 tablespoons olive oil

4 ounces thinly sliced prosciutto (or salami or pepperoni), chopped.

2 14.5-ounce cans diced tomatoes with basil, garlic, and oregano

2 14.5-ounce cans quartered artichoke hearts, drained

½ cup white wine

½ teaspoon pepper

½ cup Parmesan cheese

Follow directions on pasta package to cook linguini.

Once cooked, drain and return pasta to the pot.

As the pasta is cooking, heat oil in a large frying pan.

Add prosciutto and brown for a few minutes; stir often.

Add artichoke hearts, and cook for an additional two minutes.

Add tomatoes, wine, and pepper; stir and bring to a boil.

Reduce heat and let simmer for five more minutes.

Pour sauce over resting pasta and toss to combine.

Garnish with shredded Parmesan and season to taste.

If you've never been to the North End of Boston for Italian food, you have missed out on the experience of a lifetime! This recipe comes from the now-defunct European Restaurant, which had the best pizza and pasta in Boston.

To recreate that long-lost Boston experience at home, follow these very simple tips:

Follow the recipe exactly; do not substitute a thing!

Also, this recipe comes together quickly.

You'll want to have your ingredients measured and ready to include on the fly before you start cooking.

Mad Man Sauce

prep 10 minutes	cook 15 minutes	yields 1 quart

2 cups Kikkoman™ soy sauce
1 cup water
1½ cups cider vinegar
4 cups dark brown sugar (1 pound)
½ cup of packed, minced ginger
2 tablespoons fresh minced garlic (or more, depending on your taste)

In a saucepan, add sugar into soy sauce; stir.

Add vinegar and water; stir.

Add ginger and garlic; stir.

Heat to just short of a hard boil, then remove from heat.

Cover and let cool on stove top.

Refrigerate overnight and then strain out the solids.

This marinade keeps forever, and it's wonderful on chicken and beef.

Mama Dyer's Yankee Spin on a Southern Classic

preheat griddle	prep 2 minutes	cook 5 minutes	serves 2

4 gently stale glazed donuts (or 2 per guest)
Butter, at room temperature

This works best if the donuts are a bit stale, a day or two old.

Heat a griddle or frying pan.

With a sharp knife, slice the donut as you would a bagel.

Spread each donut half with butter and place on a hot griddle.

The goal here is to brown the donut, creating a crispy, sugary aura around the edge.

Carefully remove from the skillet (the glaze has been transformed into lava-hot molten sugar).

Place brown side down on a plate (to avoid the hot glaze from cementing the donut to the plate forever).

Let cool for a moment (if you can) and enjoy.

Serve with plenty of hot coffee or ice cold milk—and a warm, moistened napkin to keep sticky fingers nice and clean is a nice touch.

I never met Mama Dyer, and that is my loss.

She was an amazing woman who raised four boys to be wonderful husbands and fathers, and a daughter who is the most amazing woman I know.

This recipe is her classic, but beware:

The scent will send you to heaven, and the taste will make your teeth hurt, it is so sweet.

For extra decadence, try using cinnamon butter. That's how my sister-in-law makes her mama's treat all her own.

But trust me: It's worth every last calorie.

So thanks, Mama Dyer, for a job well done!

"Simple Meal" Chicken and Rice Soup

prep 30 minutes	cook 45 minutes	yield 2 quarts

1 cup of water
1 tablespoon olive oil
1 medium onion, diced
2 medium carrots, sliced
1 cup celery, sliced
3 sprigs of fresh thyme
1 bay leaf

2 quarts chicken broth
2 teaspoons minced garlic
1 cup long grain wild rice
2 cups baked chicken, shredded or cubed
Salt and pepper (to taste)

In a large stock pot, sauté the onion, carrots, celery, and herbs.

Add the garlic; stir, being careful not to let the garlic burn.

Add the chicken broth and water; stir.

When the water hits a hard boil, add the rice and chicken; stir.

Reduce heat and cover; simmer for thirty to forty-five minutes, or until rice is soft.

New England Cornbread

preheat 400°	prep 5 minutes	cook 25 minutes	yield 1 pan

1 cup unbleached AP flour
1 cup cornmeal
2 teaspoons baking powder
½ teaspoon salt
1 large egg

1 cup milk
½ cup canola oil
6 tablespoons pure maple syrup
½ cup walnuts, toasted and chopped

Spray a baking pan (8" x 8" or 9" x 9") with nonstick cooking spray.

Sift the dry ingredients together in a mixing bowl.

In another bowl, lightly turn the syrup into the egg.

Add the milk, the oil, and the egg mixture to the dry ingredients and stir until everything is combined (mixture will be slightly lumpy). Fold in the walnuts.

Pour batter into baking pan and bake for 25 minutes, or until the cornbread is browned slightly at the edges.

Indian Pudding

preheat	250°	prep	30 minutes	cook	2 hours	yield	1 large pan

6 cups milk
1 stick butter
½ cup yellow cornmeal
1/4 cup flour
1 teaspoon salt
½ cup molasses
3 eggs, beaten
1/3 cup granulated sugar
1 teaspoon of cinnamon
1 teaspoon of nutmeg
1 cup golden raisins
Whipped cream or ice cream

In either a double boiler or microwave-safe bowl, bring milk and butter to a boil; gently scald it. Keep milk hot over medium heat.

In a separate bowl, combine cornmeal, flour, and salt, then add the molasses.

Slowly thin the batter, by adding a half cup of scalded milk a few table-spoons at a time. a

Pour the thinned batter back into the pot of scalded milk. Stir continuously as the batter thickens to a soft porridge texture.

Slowly adding a half cup of the batter to the beaten eggs, whisking gently and constantly as the two are combined.

Pour the eggs and batter into the main batter pot.

Add sugar and spices; stir until smooth.

If the batter is lumpy, a hand mixer or blender can be used.

If you would like raisins, add them now.

Grease a shallow 9" x 13" baking dish; fill it with batter.

Bake at 250° for two hours, or until a toothpick inserted in the center comes out clean and dry.

To allow the flavors and textures to be their best, rest the pudding for an hour.

Serve warm with whipped cream of vanilla ice cream.

Yankee Libations

Every region of the country has a signature beverage or two, and New England has added many classic drinks to the American table.

I've gathered a few of my favorites to share.

When you're cooking up some of the food recipes in this book, why not add to the experience with a classic New England cocktail too?

Cape Codder

2 ounces vodka
2 ounces cranberry juice
Lime wedge

Sea Breeze

2 ounces vodka
1½ ounces cranberry juice
1½ ounces grapefruit juice
Lime wedge

Madras

2 parts vodka
3 parts cranberry juice
2 parts fresh orange juice
slice of orange

Dark and Stormy

5 ounces ginger beer
2 ounces dark rum
half a lime
Lime garnish

Harry's Pick-Me-Up

2 jiggers cognac
1 teaspoon grenadine syrup
juice of half a lemon
champagne
basil leaf
kosher salt

In a shaker, muddle the basil into the lemon juice.
Add ice, cognac, and grenadine syrup and shake vigorously.
Strain into a glass and top off with chilled champagne.
Add a pinch of kosher salt.

Boston Rum Punch

2 ounces dark rum
lemonade
freshly grated nutmeg
half a strawberry and a slice of orange

Fill a shaker with finely shaved or cracked ice. Add rum and lemonade and shake. Strain into a glass; garnish with nutmeg and fruit.

New England Ice Tea

1 ounce tequila
1 ounce gin
1 ounce whiskey
1 ounce white rum
1 ounce vodka
1 ounce simple syrup
Coca-Cola
orange juice

Fill a tall glass with ice.
In a shaker, combine all alcoholic ingredients and orange juice and shake to mix. Pour over ice, and top off with Coca-Cola.

Simple Syrup

1 cup sugar
1 cup water
1 teaspoon vodka (optional, used as a natural preservative)

Bring water to a boil, and add sugar. Stir until sugar dissolves and remove pan from heat. Add the vodka as a natural preservative. To prolong the syrup's shelf life, stir in the vodka (if desired) and store in the refrigerator.

Ward Eight

2 ounces rye whiskey
½ ounce lemon juice
¼ ounce orange juice
2 teaspoons grenadine syrup
maraschino cherry for garnish

Add all ingredients to a shaker and fill with ice.
Shake and strain into a martini glass; add a cherry for garnish.

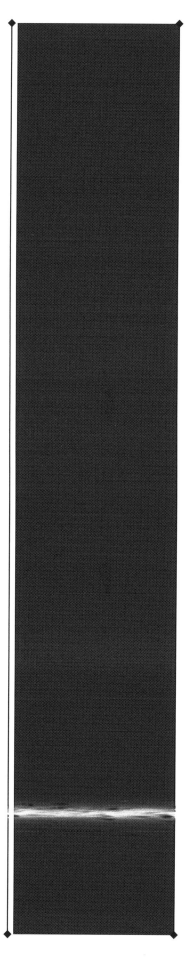

A Southerner's Guide

to Surviving Life
with Those Damn Yankees!

A Southerner's Guide to Understanding Damn Yankees

Remember when Ginger Rogers and Fred Astaire sang that great song with the "You say tom-ay-to, I say tom-ah-to" bit? Well, that happens to me here a lot. For example:

Yankees call the midday meal *lunch* and the evening meal *supper*. Southerners call their midday meal *dinner* and their evening meal … *dinner.* So don't be surprised when I show up at the wrong time when you invite me to dinner! When extending such an invitation to a Yankee, it would be a true kindness to add a time to help the poor creature plan accordingly.

Yankees say, "I am getting ready to leave." Southerners say, "I am fixin' to leave." It took me forever to figure out what they were trying to *fix.*

When Yankee Bostonians ask for a "tonic," they could be asking for any carbonated beverage—a Coke or a root beer or a Moxie. You just need to ask what *kind* of tonic we'd like. To us, it's all just tonic. On the other hand, a *tonic* is something a Southerner drinks to cure what ails them (or maybe mixes with gin; same thing).

Yankees call them *peanuts.* Southerners call them *goober peas*—and they BOIL them!

Yankees say, "What a moron!" when someone does something stupid.
Southerners say, "Bless their heart!" Another local euphemism it took me forever to decipher!

I'll be the first to admit that there are days I think you folks must think I'm from another planet, not just a state north of the Mason-Dixon Line. I talk funny. I think … differently from most of y'all. I'm known to be, as y'all say, *contrary.* But at my core, I know we're not all that different, so I've got a good notion to make you understand how we Northerners tick.

Yankees are an independent group, forged by generations in the cold, harsh, barren tundra known as New England. (Well, that's what a lot of Southerners think, anyway.) Actually, the weather in New England is pleasant enough, part of the year. A quick comparison reveals that:

You have your blast-furnace summers | We have our blast-furnace summers

You have gray, cold, rainy winters | We have gray, cold, rainy winters

You have hurricanes |We have nor'easters

I guess the key to "understanding" Damn Yankees is simple:

Even though we make talk "funny" to you or think "different" from you, we're all just doing our best to make it through the day. The Yankee/Southerner translations are still being worked out, on both sides. So the next time some Yankee does something that befuddles you or gets you all tore up, invite them to set for a spell and enjoy some sweet tea and supper with you—just as I would hope a Yankee might do if you wandered up into their mysterious lands.

Bout the South: Southern Humor

Please Don't Try This at Home, Kids

As I was talking about writing my own cookbook, a friend shared a hilarious gag recipe with me, and I had to share it with you. Apparently, circulating around the Internet is a recipe for making a perfect turkey. All you do is stuff the cavity with uncooked popcorn. Popcorn as a stuffing ingredient? Imagine that. When I found this recipe, I thought it was perfect for people like me, who just are not sure how to tell when a turkey is thoroughly cooked, but not dried out.

Can you imagine? After about four hours, the recipe instructed people to listen for the popping sounds. When the turkey's ass blows the oven door open and the bird flies across the room, it's done. As I said, please don't try this one at home!

Confuse-A-Yankee, Disaster Edition

One of the funniest stories I heard recently was about a young reporter from a New England newspaper who came to the South to do a human interest story following the terrible tragedy of the 2011 Tuscaloosa, Alabama, tornado. As she toured the devastation, she was struck by how many houses of worship had been destroyed, and thought this may make a good story. Having been told of the friendliness of Southerners, she stopped a middle-aged woman standing in front of a decimated home.

In her fine Yankee accent, the young reporter said to the woman "I've noticed the terrible destruction here, especially the churches. How has that affected you?"

"Not too much," the woman replied, not missing a beat. "I have been going to Popeye's for years."

At which point the woman walked away, leaving the young reporter completely at a loss.

(Right now, the Southerners are laughing, and the Yankees don't get it—and that's okay).

A Sighting of a Rare and Endangered Species in These Here Parts

Shortly after we moved to Tennessee, my sister- and brother-in-law from Indiana came to visit. I decided to throw a small cocktail party to welcome them on their first visit. We invited a few of our new local friends and neighbors over. Imagine my distress when one pair of neighbors strolled in, took one look at our visiting family members, and said without the slightest hint of irony (or manners), "Are those the lib-rulls?"

I had the good grace to be horrified, but my family had the good *sense* not to be offended. (In some odd way, I suspect that it's even some weird badge of honor in their eyes.) We still laugh about this to this day, but man, was that an eye-opener for a newly transplanted Yankee!

FOOD FOR THOUGHT:

A TASTE OF THE SOUTH

or

How a Yankee Learned to Cook

Like Y'all Do

So, for you Yankees who have never been able to experience life in the South, its culture, and food, here are a few recipes to broaden your culinary horizons.

Go ahead, be brave, and give them a try.

Why not plan a Southern party? I have a whole menu here (and don't you dare forget the sweet tea)!

I'll start with one of MY favorite new foods, a truly *Southern* dish. (And you thought was only made in Vermont!)

prep 5 minutes	yield 2 ⅔ cups

2 cups shredded extra-sharp cheddar cheese
8 ounces cream cheese, softened
½ cup mayonnaise
¼ teaspoon garlic powder
¼ teaspoon ground cayenne pepper (optional)
¼ teaspoon onion powder
1 jalapeno pepper, seeded and minced (optional)
1 4-ounce jar diced pimentos, drained
salt and black pepper to taste

Place all ingredients into a large mixing bowl.

Beat at medium speed, with paddle if possible, until thoroughly combined.

Season to taste with salt and black pepper.

Spread on crackers, use as a vegetable dip, or for an extremely decadent treat, use it to make grilled cheese sandwiches.

Redneck Caviar

prep 5 minutes	*chill* 4 hours	*yield* 8 cups

1 14-ounce can whole kernel corn
1 14-ounce can diced tomatoes
1 14-ounce can black beans
1 14-ounce can black-eyed peas
1 medium green bell pepper, finely chopped
1 medium onion, finely chopped
1 8-ounce bottle of Italian dressing
tortilla chips

Using a large colander over the sink, drain and rinse all canned vegetables.

Chop onion and green pepper into small pieces.

Transfer all vegetables in a large mixing bowl.

Add Italian dressing; stir to combine.

Cover and chill for several hours.

This pretty little dish will generate a ton of compliments—and as many requests for the recipe.

The good news is that it's as simple to make as it is delicious. It's also a bright, beautiful, and healthy alternative for entertaining or snacking.

And it's a great way to get folks like me (who hate vegetables) to actually enjoy them!

Fried Green Tomatoes

preheat oil to 350°	prep 10 minutes	cook 10 to 15 minutes	yield 20 slices

4 large green tomatoes
2 eggs
½ cup milk
1 cup all-purpose flour
½ cup cornmeal
½ cup bread crumbs
2 teaspoons coarse kosher salt
¼ teaspoon ground black pepper
1 quart vegetable oil (for frying)

Slice tomatoes evenly. I like my slices nice and thin (¼") but I've seen these cut as thick as ½"; it's your choice. Just adjust the cooking time if you like thicker slices.

In a medium bowl, whisk eggs and milk together.

In a second plate (or pie pan), stir flour, cornmeal, and seasonings to combine.

Whisk eggs and milk together in a medium-size bowl. Scoop flour onto a plate.

To bread the slices, start by giving them with a light coating of the flour/cornmeal mixture. Then dip into the egg and milk wash, and finish with a final dip into the flour/cornmeal mixture for a nice, crispy coating.

In a large, heavy skillet, add ½" of oil and bring to 350°.

Check that the oil is at the proper temperature; adjust as necessary.

Carefully place tomatoes into the oil, in small batches. Do not crowd the tomatoes or allow them to touch, or they won't brown properly.

Fry until golden brown, turning the slices once to ensure even cooking.

Drain on paper towels and serve immediately!

Fried Dill Pickles

preheat oil to 350°	prep 10 minutes	cook 10 to 15 minutes	yield 20 slices

½ cup buttermilk
salt and black pepper to taste
1 jar dill pickle slices
½ cup all-purpose flour
1 ½ cups fine cornmeal
1 teaspoon seafood seasoning, such
as Old Bay™
¼ teaspoon Cajun seasoning
1 quart oil for frying

Pickle Dippin' Sauce
½ teaspoon Cajun seasoning
1 jar buttermilk ranch dressing

In a small bowl, combine the buttermilk ranch dressing and ½ teaspoon of the Cajun seasoning; stir to combine. Set aside.

In a large, heavy skillet, add ½" of oil and bring to 350°.

Cover a plate with parchment paper or wax paper.

In a shallow dish, combine buttermilk, salt, and pepper.

Place pickles in mixture and set aside.

In a gallon zipper bag, combine flour, cornmeal, seafood seasoning, and ¼ teaspoon of the Cajun seasoning; shake to mix well.

Add pickles a few at a time to the bag; tumble gently to coat evenly with the flour mixture.

Remove from bag, shaking any extra flour off, and place on prepared plate.

Check that the oil is at the proper temperature; adjust as necessary.

Carefully lower the pickles in the oil, in small batches. Do not crowd the pickles or allow them to touch, or they won't brown properly.

Fry for one to two minutes, or until the coating is a rich, golden brown; turning the slices to ensure that they cook evenly.

And since we are completely uninterested in controlling our cholesterol, we may as well try out another Southern classic.

This one is as Southern as they come—which is probably why it will have my New York Jewish deli lovers apoplectic!

Proper Southern Grits

prep 5 minutes	cook 10 to 15 minutes	yield 1 cup

3 cups water
½ teaspoon salt
1 cup hominy grits
freshly ground black pepper to taste
1 tablespoon butter
½ cup shredded sharp cheddar cheese

In a medium saucepan, add water and salt; bring to a boil.

To avoid clumps, add grits, whisking as you add them to the boiling water.

Continue to whisk as the mixture returns to a boil and the mixture is smooth.

Reduce heat to low, and cook for 10 to 15 minutes, stirring frequently.

When the grits are fully cooked, remove from heat and stir in cheese, spices, and butter.

Stir until all ingredients are combined and the cheese is melted.

In the South, no meal is complete without a steaming side of grits.

What impresses this Yankee is how creative Southerners are when it comes to keeping grits interesting. If they're looking for something savory, they'll add all sort of things, like cheese, crumbled bacon or sausage, corn, green chili, or hot sauce.

If they're craving sweet grits, I've seen folks stir in sugar, jam, maple syrup, or berries.

But the one constant that everyone uses, in every version, is butter.

Lot and LOTS of butter.

This is a good, basic recipe for making cheesy grits.

Enjoy!

Southern Sweet Potato Casserole

| prep 15 minutes | cook 75 minutes | serves 8 |

6 large sweet potatoes
2 sticks salted butter
2 cups white sugar
1 teaspoon ground cinnamon
1 teaspoon ground nutmeg
1 tablespoon vanilla extract
salt to taste

Peel the sweet potatoes and cut them into slices.

Melt the butter or margarine in a heavy skillet and add the sliced sweet potatoes.

Mix the sugar, cinnamon, nutmeg and salt. Cover the sweet potatoes with sugar mixture and stir.

Cover skillet, reduce heat to low and cook for about 1 hour or until potatoes are "candied." They should be tender but still a little hard around the edges.

As it cooks, the sauce should turn a nice, rich caramel color. To keep it from burning, you need to keep an eye on it and keep it moving; stir occasionally.

Stir in the vanilla just before serving.

Serve hot.

"But Kate," my impatient reader is certainly asking, "these Southern recipes are all well and good ... but *where* is your fried chicken recipe?"

To that, I say, "All good things come to those who wait."

So, before we get to the main attraction, it's time to highlight a few classic Southern side dishes. Of course, you can't have chicken without some calorie-laden starches. Most Yankees would add French fries or mashed potatoes, but no self-respecting Southerner ever would!

For the record, sweet potatoes are the *only* acceptable potato to go with fried chicken (at least according to my fried chicken-loving friend).

Luckily for us, she also wanted to share her favorite sweet potato recipe as well.

Collard Greens for New Year's Day

prep 10 minutes	cook 3 hours	serves 8

1½ quarts water
1½ pounds ham hocks
4 pounds collard greens, rinsed and trimmed
½ teaspoon crushed red pepper flakes (optional)
¼ cup vegetable oil
salt and pepper to taste

In a large pot with a tight-fitting lid, bring the ham hock and water to a boil.

Reduce the heat, and simmer (covered) for 30 minutes.

Add the collards and the hot pepper flakes the pot; stir.

Replace the cover and let it simmer for about 2 hours, remembering to stir the pot occasionally.

Add the vegetable oil and stir.

Replace the cover and let it simmer for a final 30 minutes.

Hoppin' John

prep 15 minutes	cook 1 hour	serves 8

1 tablespoon extra virgin olive oil
1 large ham hock (or bacon, sausage, or ham)
1 cup onion
¾ cup celery
¾ cup green pepper
1 tablespoon garlic
1 bag of black-eyed peas

1 quart chicken stock
3 tablespoons green onion
1 bay leaf
1 teaspoon thyme
4 tablespoons canola oil
Salt, black pepper, cayenne, and hot sauce (to taste)
3 cups steamed white rice

DON'T FORGET TO PLAN AHEAD! The night before you plan to serve, transfer the dried peas to a large bowl. Add enough water to cover the peas and soak them overnight.

Chop all vegetables into a small cubes and set aside.

Add canola oil to a large, heavy soup pot and heat over medium-high heat.

Sear the ham hock (or alternate meat) until a nice crust is formed on all sides; reduce heat.

Add the vegetables and garlic, and cook for five minutes.

Drain the water from the peas, rinse them well, and add to the pot.

Add the stock, herbs, and seasonings; stir and bring back to a boil.

Reduce the heat and simmer for 40 minutes, stirring occasionally. If the liquid evaporates, add more water or stock.

As the Hoppin' John is cooking, prepare rice according to package directions.

Serve over rice and garnish with green onions.

In the South, Hoppin' John is another treasured culinary tradition to ring a new year.

Eating this dish is said to bring a year's worth of good luck, health, and prosperity— and it's damn tasty too!

Buttermilk Hush Puppies

preheat oil to 200°	*prep* 10 minutes	*cook* two to five minutes	*makes* 36 to 40

½ cup vegetable oil
4 eggs at room temperature
2 cups cornmeal
2½ cups all-purpose white flour
¼ cup sugar (optional)
1 teaspoon baking soda
1 teaspoon salt
¾ cup onions, minced

8 green onions, minced
2 cups buttermilk

Optional stir-in ideas: ¼ cup corn; 1 jalapeño pepper (seeded and diced); Cajun seasoning.

Vegetable oil (for frying)

In a deep fryer or large, deep, heavy saucepan, bring vegetable oil to 365°.

In a large mixing bowl, combine buttermilk, ½ cup of the vegetable oil, and eggs.

In a separate bowl, whisk the cornmeal, flour, baking soda, salt, and sugar together. Add the onions and green onions and mix until just incorporated. If you like corn, add it. If you like heat, add in some jalapeño pepper pieces.

Carefully drop tablespoon-sized batter balls into the hot oil and fry until golden brown (about 6 to 10 minutes)

Remove the cooked hush puppies with a slotted spoon and place on brown paper bags or paper towels to drain.

To keep them warm until ready to serve, transfer the cooked hush puppies to a baking sheet in the oven.

True Southern-Style Cole Slaw

prep	10 minutes	chill	at least two hours

6 cups cabbage, shredded

1 carrot, shredded

¾ cup mayonnaise

2 tablespoons white vinegar (or to taste)

2 tablespoons vegetable oil

2½ tablespoons sugar (or to taste)

½ teaspoon celery salt

1/4 teaspoon salt (or to taste)

In a large mixing bowl, toss the shredded cabbage and carrots; mix well.

In a smaller bowl, combine the mayonnaise, vinegar, vegetable oil, sugar, salt, and celery salt. Taste, and adjust seasonings as needed. If it's too tart, add more sugar. Conversely, if it's too sweet, add more vinegar.

Once you are satisfied with the dressing, pour it into the larger bowl and stir until all the vegetables are evenly coated.

For best flavor and texture, refrigerate for at least two hours.

Every region of the country has its own version of cole slaw, but I think the Southerners make some of the best. It's rich, creamy, and tangy.

I can't get enough of this stuff.

Cole slaw only gets better with time; it needs to marinate and find its balance. For that reason, making it the day before can be a really good idea (and that makes it one thing off your last-minute to-do list before guests arrive).

Oh-So-Southern White Beans

prep 15 minutes	cook 2 hours	serves 8 to 10

16 ounces of dried navy beans *(soaked overnight)*

8 to 10 cups of water

1 ham bone or hock

1 white or red onion, chopped

1 tablespoon (or two cloves) garlic, chopped

1 teaspoon sugar

1 teaspoon black pepper

1 tablespoon Cajun seasoning

2 bay leaves

DON'T FORGET TO PLAN AHEAD! The night before you plan to serve, transfer the dried beans to a large bowl. Add enough water to cover the beans and soak them overnight.

Place the ham bone or ham hock in a large Dutch oven or soup pot, cover with water, and bring to a boil.

Reduce heat to a simmer (or transfer everything to a slow cooker on low), and add the remaining ingredients; stir to combine.

If finishing on the stovetop, simmer for two hours (or until beans are tender).

If finishing in the slow cooker, set on low. Check periodically throughout the day to make sure the liquid is not reducing too quickly.

You can eat this either as a side dish as is or as a soup—just add a bit more water until you reach the desired consistency.

Remove the cooked hush puppies with a slotted spoon and place on brown paper bags or paper towels to drain.

To keep them warm until ready to serve, transfer the cooked hush puppies to a baking sheet in the oven.

How many Southern children grew up with these hearty little white beans as part of their diet? Most, I think, based on what folks I've spoken to have said.

If you're looking for a filling, tasty, and affordable dinner, a bowl of piping hot white beans with a slab of cornbread is heaven on Earth.

The best part? This dish is perfect for a slow cooker. You'll need to start this on the stovetop, but the contents can then be transferred to the slow cooker to finish.

Set it up in the morning on low, and by dinner, you'll have a simple feast on your hands.

Decadent Southern Macaroni & Cheese

preheat	350°	prep	30 minutes	cook	1 hour	serves	8 to 10

1½ teaspoons kosher salt (or to taste)
8 ounces elbow macaroni
7 ounces (or 1 ½ cups) extra-sharp Cheddar cheese, cubed
7 ounces (or 1 ½ cups) extra sharp Cheddar cheese, grated
2½ tablespoons white flour
1½ teaspoons dry mustard
¼ teaspoon black pepper

¼ teaspoon nutmeg, freshly grated
¼ teaspoon cayenne pepper
¾ cup sour cream
2 eggs, lightly beaten
1½ cups half-and-half
1½ cups heavy cream
¼ cup grated onion
1 teaspoon Worcestershire sauce
butter (to grease the pan)

Bring four quarts of water to boil in a large soup pan and add pasta.

Cook for three to four minutes, then remove from heat.

Drain and rinse the pasta, and transfer to a 9" x 13" baking dish that has been coated with butter.

Stir in the cubed cheese and stir well.

In a large mixing bowl, combine salt, flour, dry mustard, black pepper, nutmeg, and cayenne; stir well.

In a small mixing bowl, combine the sour cream and the eggs; stir well.

To the egg mixture, add the onions, half-and-half, heavy cream, and Worcestershire sauce; stir to combine.

Pour the egg and cream mixture over the pasta and cheese; stir until all the pasta is coated.

Reduce heat to a simmer (or transfer everything to a slow cooker on low), and add the remaining ingredients; stir to combine.

Sprinkle the shredded cheddar over the top of the pasta and put the pan in the oven.

Bake for about one hour, or until the pasta mixture begins to set up a little around the edges and the cheese turns a nice, golden brown.

Remove from oven and let it rest for ten minutes before serving.

Okay, I'll admit that this seemingly simple dish is one of the more complicated in the collection … but man, is it worth it!

It's creamy, cheesy, savory, satisfying, and wonderful. This is how professional chefs make real macaroni and cheese.

Once you try it, you'll think twice about reaching for that little blue box ever again. If you liked my Turtle Noodles, you must try this recipe too!

Make this up in huge batches; it freezes really well.

It ain't health food, but like Mama Dyer's donuts, it's worth every single calorie.

This is comfort food, defined.

Southerners love their fried food, and with good reason.

It's delicious, and they have perfected the technique.

Few things are more "Southern" than fried Catfish and once you try it, you'll understand the passion.

Fried catfish is a Southern tradition, along with buttermilk hush puppies, coleslaw, and white beans!

Southern Fried Catfish

preheat oil to 350°	*prep* 10 minutes	*cook* 20 minutes	*yield* 1 pound

½ cup buttermilk
½ cup water
1 pound catfish fillets, cut in strips
1½ cups fine cornmeal
½ cup all-purpose flour
1 teaspoon seafood seasoning, such as Old Bay™ Seasoning
Salt and pepper (to taste)
1 quart vegetable oil for deep frying

In a large skillet (preferably cast iron), bring vegetable oil to 350°.

In a large plastic bag, combine the dry breading ingredients (flour, cornmeal, Old Bay Seasoning, and salt, and pepper). Shake well to mix thoroughly.

In a large bowl, combine the buttermilk, water, and salt and pepper.

Pour milk mixture into a baking dish large enough to hold all of the filets.

Place the fish in the pan, turning each filet over once to coat with milk; set aside to marinate for 15 minutes.

Pour the milk mixture over the fish and set aside to marinate.

Remove each piece of fish from the milk and then put it, one by one, into the flour mixture in the bag. Seal the bag and shake to coat.

Once all the fish is ready to fry, carefully place it in the hot oil.

Fry until the edges are brown and the batter is a golden brown (approximately three minutes per side). The fish should be crispy on the outside and flaky on the inside.

Use a meat thermometer to confirm that the internal temperature has reached 150°.

Remove from oil and drain on paper towels.

Keep cooked fish warm on a baking dish in a 200° oven.

Southern Fried Chicken

preheat oil to 350°	prep 10 minutes	cook 20 minutes	yield 1 pound

¾ cup all-purpose flour
¾ cup grated Parmesan cheese
1½ cups bread crumbs
1 teaspoon poultry seasoning
½ teaspoon onion powder
½ teaspoon garlic powder
½ teaspoon salt

½ teaspoon pepper
1½ cups milk
12 ounces chicken tenderloins
1 quart vegetable oil for frying

In a large skillet (preferably cast iron), bring vegetable oil to 350°.

In a large plastic bag, combine the dry breading ingredients (flour, Parmesan cheese, bread crumbs, poultry seasoning, onion powder, garlic powder, and salt and pepper. Shake well to mix thoroughly.

Pour the milk into a large bowl.

For the best results, each piece of chicken must be breaded individually. This is not the place to rush the process!

Dip each piece of chicken into the milk and then put it into the flour mixture in the bag. Seal the bag and shake to coat.

Repeat this two-step process for each piece of chicken. (If you like it extra crispy, double batter each piece.) Place breaded chicken on a holding plate until you are ready to cook.

Once all the chicken is ready to fry, carefully place it in the hot oil.

Fry until the edges are brown, and then flip them over to cook. Larger pieces like breasts need about fifteen minutes to cook thoroughly, so start these first.

Use a meat thermometer to confirm that the internal temperature has reached 180°.

Remove from oil and drain on paper towels.

Keep cooked chicken warm on a baking dish in a 200° oven.

Nothing says "Southern cooking" quite like fried chicken. Just ask Paula Deen!

(And no, this isn't her recipe. You can find that anywhere.)

What I *am* giving you is a something even better: A family recipe reluctantly shared by a fine Southern lady whose name must be kept a secret!

She says that she would be skinned alive for giving her family's fried chicken recipe ... *to a Yankee!*

Horrors!

So to this fine lady, I say "thank you" from all us Yankees for the privilege of eating your chicken!

Melt-in-Your-Mouth Southern Biscuits

preheat 450°	prep 15 minutes	cook 12 to 15 minutes	yield 6

1½ cups all-purpose flour

1½ teaspoons sugar

1½ teaspoons baking powder

¾ teaspoon salt

½ cup shortening

½ teaspoon baking soda

⅔ cup buttermilk (or if you prefer regular milk, omit the baking soda)

1 tablespoon butter, melted

In a large mixing bowl, combine flour, sugar, baking powder, salt, and baking soda.

Cut the shortening in until the mixture is reduced to fine clumps.

Slowly start to add the buttermilk and stir. You'll know you've added enough when the dough pulls away from the side of the bowl and starts to form a ball. (If this doesn't happen, keep adding more buttermilk a tablespoon at a time until you reach the desired consistency.)

Turn dough out onto a floured surface and knead until smooth. Be careful not to overwork the dough or biscuits could be tough.

Roll (or pat) the dough to an even ¾" in height, cut the individual biscuits with a 2½" cutter, and place them on a greased cookie sheet. If you like crusty sides, place them about an inch apart. If you like soft sides, have them lightly touch on the sheet.

Brush the tops with melted butter.

Bake for 12 to 15 minutes, or until they are a rich, golden brown.

Remove from cookie sheet immediately.

Serve these with honey and warm butter so they are certain to literally melt in your mouth.

Southern-Style Buttermilk Biscuits

| preheat 450° | prep 15 minutes | cook 12 to 15 minutes | yield 10 |

2 cups all-purpose Southern-style white flour
2½ teaspoons baking powder
¼ teaspoon baking soda
1 teaspoon salt
¼ cup lard (or vegetable shortening), well chilled
2 tablespoons butter, well chilled
¾ cup buttermilk

Move oven rack to the center position, and heat to 450°.

In a large mixing bowl, combine flour, baking powder, soda, and salt; stir to combine.

Cut in chilled shortening and butter until you have pieces the size of small peas.

In the bowl, create a well in the center of the dry ingredients. Pour the buttermilk into the well.

Using a wooden spoon, gently incorporate the dry ingredients into the buttermilk until the mixture just starts to clump together. If it's too dry, add a little more buttermilk as needed.

Turn the dough out onto a lightly floured surface and pat or roll until the dough is approximately ½" tall.

Cut biscuits as desired (this recipe will make 10 to 12 three-inch biscuits) and place onto an ungreased cookie sheet.

Bake for 10 to 12 minutes, or until biscuits are a rich, golden brown

Transfer biscuits immediately to a cloth-lined basket and serve with butter, honey, jam, or apple butter.

Buttermilk makes anything better, and biscuits are no exception to that rule.

Buttermilk adds a subtle, bright tanginess to the end product, and I think it makes them taste creamier too.

So here are two classic spins on the classic Southern biscuit, a cherished crown jewel of Southern cuisine.

Both use buttermilk, but they produce subtle differences in flavor and texture.

Why not try them both?

Peach Cobbler

preheat 425°	prep 15 minutes	cook 45 minutes	serves 8

FILLING:
8 fresh peaches, sliced
¼ cup white sugar
¼ cup brown sugar
¼ teaspoon ground cinnamon
⅛ teaspoon ground nutmeg
1 teaspoon fresh lemon juice
2 teaspoons cornstarch

COBBLER:
1 cup all-purpose flour

¼ cup white sugar
¼ cup brown sugar
1 teaspoon baking powder
½ teaspoon salt
6 tablespoons unsalted butter, chilled and cut into small pieces
¼ cup boiling water

SPRINKLES:
3 tablespoons white sugar
1 teaspoon ground cinnamon

Grease a 2-quart baking dish; set aside.

In a large bowl, combine liquid ingredients for filling (white sugar, brown sugar, cinnamon, nutmeg, lemon juice, and cornstarch); stir to combine.

Add peaches and gently turn glaze around the slices.

Pour peach mixture into the baking dish and place on middle rack of oven.

Bake at 425° for 10 minutes. As the filling is baking, prepare the cobbler dough.

In a large mixing bowl, combine dry ingredients for cobbler (flour, white sugar, brown sugar, baking powder, and salt). Stir to combine.

Using your hands or a pastry blender, incorporate the butter. The finished mixture should resemble coarse meal with pea-sized chunks of butter.

Add water to dough mix until it just starts to come together. Do not overwork it, or the crust can be heavy.

Remove baking dish from oven and add cobbler mix by dropping hearty dollops directly on the top of the hot peach filling.

In a small dish, prepare the sprinkles by combining sugar and cinnamon; dust cobbler dough with this mixture.

Return baking dish to oven and bake until cobbler pieces are a rich, golden brown (about 30 minutes).

Pecan Pie

| preheat 350° | prep 15 minutes | cook 55 to 60 minutes | serves 8 |

1 cup light corn syrup
3 tablespoons butter
½ cup firmly packed light brown sugar
2 tablespoon all-purpose flour
¼ teaspoon salt
3 eggs, lightly beaten
1½ teaspoons vanilla extract
1½ cups coarsely chopped pecans
1 9" frozen, deep-dish pie shell, thawed

In a large saucepan, over medium heat, combine corn syrup, butter, brown sugar, flour, and salt; stir until butter melts; remove from heat.

In a small bowl, combine eggs and vanilla; stir well.

Add pecans; stir well.

Pour filling into uncooked pie shell.

Carefully transfer pie plate to a baking sheet (to contain any spills) and place on the middle rack of the oven.

Bake for 55 to 60 minutes or until filling sets up.

Well, to be fair, when you're in the South, you will have no shortage of decadent, sweet treats to finish your dining experience.

This is one of the sweetest, most Southern dishes I can imagine. It's too sweet for some, but others can't get enough.

This is one of these surprisingly simple, yet spectacular, desserts. Looking to impress a hostess?

Show up with one of these tasty showstoppers and you'll be guaranteed more dinner Invitations.

HINT:
Save time and hassle by using a frozen pie crust; no one will notice because what it holds is so wonderful.

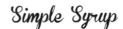

Southern Libations

So, after that fine Southern meal, sit back, stretch out and relax with a cold glass of sweet tea, or better yet, Kentucky bourbon or Tennessee whiskey.

Just as Yankees have their signature cocktails, the Southerners have also created some of the most delicious and refreshing concoctions ever to challenge a bartender.

Simple Syrup

1 cup sugar
1 cup water
1 teaspoon vodka (optional, used as a natural preservative)

Bring water to a boil, and add sugar. Stir until sugar dissolves and remove pan from heat. Add the vodka as a natural preservative. To prolong the syrup's shelf life, stir in the vodka (if desired) and store in the refrigerator.

Southern Sweet Tea

1 ounce loose-leaf black tea
1 quart water (boiling)
1 quart water (room temperature)
simple syrup (to taste)

Infuse the tea leaves into hot water for four minutes; strain into pitcher filled with room-temperature water. Add simple syrup to taste, and serve over ice.

Mint Juleps

2 cups water
2 cups sugar
¼ cup mint leaves, chopped
4 ounces Kentucky bourbon
1 sprig fresh mint

In a saucepan, bring water, sugar, and chopped mint leaves to a boil. Boil until the sugar is completely dissolved; remove from heat. Allow to cool thoroughly and remove the mint with a fine strainer. Fill eight chilled silver cups or glasses with crushed ice. Pour 4 ounces of Kentucky bourbon and ¼ of the mint syrup into each. Garnish with mint springs and serve. Makes 8 cocktails.

Tiger Paw

1 ounce Southern Comfort liqueur
1 ounce pineapple juice
1 ounce raspberry wine

Combine all ingredients in a cocktail shaker until well blended. Strain into a martini glass and garnish with fruit if desired.

Old-Fashioned

2 tablespoons simple syrup (or 1 sugar cube)
1 teaspoon water
2 dashes bitters
1½ ounces of bourbon
1 slice orange
1 maraschino cherry
2 cups sugar

Pour the syrup, water, and bitters into a whiskey glass; stir to combine.
Fill glass with ice and add bourbon.
Stir and garnish with orange slice and cherry.

Tennessee Tornado

1 ounce sloe gin
1 ounce Southern Comfort liqueur
1 ounce triple sec liqueur
1 ounce Galliano
6 ounces orange juice
2 maraschino cherries
1 slice of orange

Combine all ingredients in a cocktail shaker until well blended.
Strain into a martini glass and garnish with fruit if desired.

Vanilla Lemonade

4 lemons
½ cup sugar
¼ teaspoon vanilla extract
4 ounces vanilla vodka (optional)
6 cups cold water

Cut the lemons in half and scoop the pulp into a blender. Add have the rinds
along with the sugar, vanilla, and 2 cups of the water. Blend until smooth, then
strain into a serving pitcher. Add the remaining water and serve.

Peach-Bourbon Sours

½ cup peach preserves
½ cup hot water
1 cup bourbon
3 tablespoons lemon juice

In a glass pitcher, whisk together the peach preserves and the hot water. Stir
until the preserves are dissolved. Add bourbon and lemon juice and whisk to
combine. Fill a cocktail shaker with ice and add one-third of the liquid.
Shake until thoroughly chilled, pour over ice. Makes six 12-ounce servings.

So That's All for Now, Friends!

I hope you enjoyed reading this little missive as much as I enjoyed writing it.

I left space at the end of each recipe for you to add you own favorites,
be they Yankee, Southern, or somewhere in between.

We may all live in the same country,
but when it comes to food,
we are continents apart!

I hope this little book made you smile some,
enlightened you a bit about life in another part of the country,
gave you a few good recipes, and generally made you happy for a few minutes.

Thanks to all who shared their memories,
helpful hints, insights, recipes, and skills to make this happen:

Dana Dyer Pierson
who so wonderfully shaped and designed this book
(and gave me the idea for the cover).

Joel Pierson
who made it all happen at the publishing end.

Mary McRae
who gave me three of her mama's favorite Southern recipes.

And
the fine people of Cheatham County, Tennessee,
who have made these last eight years the time of my life.
Thanks for all the Southern hospitality.

I couldn't have done it without you!

And to the Yankees who raised and formed me
and the Southerners who have accepted me,
my eternal thanks and appreciation!

As the song says, "May we all live together in peace."

—Kate

Recipe Index